LE CORDON BLEU

HOME COLLECTION

·SOUPS·

MURDOCH BOOKS®

Sydney • London • Vancouver • New York

contents

recipe ratings ✹ *easy* ✹✹ *a little more care needed* ✹✹✹ *more care needed*

French onion soup

Known in France as Soupe à l'oignon gratinée, French onion soup has always been a very popular first course during a cold winter in Paris.

Preparation time 20 minutes
Total cooking time 1 hour 5 minutes
Serves 6

45 g (1 1/2 oz) unsalted butter
1 small red onion, finely sliced
400 g (12 3/4 oz) white onions, finely sliced
1 clove garlic, finely chopped
25 g (3/4 oz) plain flour
200 ml (6 1/2 fl oz) white wine
1.5 litres brown stock (see page 63) or water
bouquet garni (see page 63)
1 tablespoon sherry

CROUTES
12 slices of French baguette
200 g (6 1/2 oz) Gruyère cheese, finely grated

1 Melt the butter in a large heavy-based pan over medium heat. Add the onions and cook for 20 minutes, stirring often, until caramelised and dark golden-brown.

This step is very important as the colour of the onions at this stage will determine the colour of the final soup. Stir in the garlic and the flour and cook, stirring continuously, for 1–2 minutes.

2 Add the white wine and stir the mixture until the flour has blended in smoothly. Bring to the boil slowly, stirring continuously. Whisk or briskly stir in the stock or water, add the bouquet garni, and season with salt and freshly ground black pepper. Simmer gently for about 30 minutes, then skim the surface of excess fat if necessary. Add the sherry to the soup and adjust the seasoning to taste.

3 To make the croutes, toast the bread slices until dry and golden on both sides.

4 Ladle the soup into warm bowls and float the croutes on top of each one. Sprinkle with the grated Gruyère cheese and place under a preheated grill until the cheese melts and becomes lightly golden brown. Serve the soup immediately.

Chef's tip The flour can be omitted if a lighter soup texture is desired.

Cream of leek and orange soup

A delicious puréed leek and potato soup, topped with a spoonful of orange and Cointreau cream and browned under the grill.

Preparation time **30 minutes**
Total cooking time **55 minutes**
Serves 4

30 g (1 oz) unsalted butter
500 g (1 lb) leeks, white part only, thinly sliced
250 g (8 oz) potatoes, thinly sliced
1 litre chicken stock (see page 62)
300 ml (10 fl oz) cream
finely grated rind of 1 orange
1 tablespoon Cointreau
200 ml (6¹/₂ fl oz) cream, for whipping
fresh chervil leaves, to garnish

1 Melt the butter in a large stockpot over low heat. Add the leek with a pinch of salt and cook slowly for about 10 minutes, or until the leeks are soft.
2 Add the potato and cook for 3 minutes, then pour in the stock. Bring to the boil and simmer for 20 minutes. Add the cream and cook for another 10 minutes. Using a blender or food processor, purée the soup until smooth. Season with salt and black pepper to taste and keep warm.
3 Preheat the grill and mix the orange rind and Cointreau in a small bowl. In a separate bowl, beat the whipping cream until stiff peaks form. Fold into the grated orange and Cointreau.
4 Ladle the soup into bowls and top with a spoonful of the orange cream. Place under the grill until just brown. Scatter with a few leaves of chervil and some freshly ground black pepper.

Seafood and lemon soup

The tang of lemon is refreshing and highly complementary to the richness of the seafood.
A very elegant and refined dish.

*Preparation time **25 minutes***
*Total cooking time **20 minutes***
*Serves **6–8***

400 g (12³/4 oz) cockles or pipis
500 g (1 lb) small mussels
400 g (12³/4 oz) clams
100 ml (3¹/4 fl oz) dry white wine
3 French shallots, finely chopped
6 scallops (ask your fishmonger to open the shells,
 remove the scallops and trim them)
2 small squid (ask your fishmonger to skin the squid
 and prepare them for cooking)
300 ml (10 fl oz) fish stock (see page 62)
100 ml (3¹/4 fl oz) cream
20 g (³/4 oz) chilled unsalted butter, cut into cubes
1 small carrot, cut into julienne strips (see Chef's tip)
1 celery stick, cut into julienne strips
¹/2 leek, cut into julienne strips
100 g (3¹/4 oz) small cooked prawns, peeled
finely grated rind of 1 lemon
chopped fresh chervil or parsley, to garnish

1 Wash the cockles or pipis, mussels and clams in lots of water and repeat twice. Be especially careful with the cockles or pipis, they can be very sandy. Place the shellfish in a large pot with the wine and shallots, bring the mixture slowly to the boil and cook for 2–3 minutes, or until the shells open. Lift the shellfish out of the cooking liquid, remove the flesh from the shells and set aside. It may be necessary to wash any sandy cockles or pipis again.

2 Add the scallops to the cooking liquid and poach for 1–3 minutes, then remove and cut into small cubes. Cut the squid into small cubes and fry in a pan with a little hot oil, drain on crumpled paper towels and set aside.

3 Pour the cooking liquid from the shellfish into a clean pan and add the fish stock and cream. Place over high heat and boil for 3–5 minutes, or until a very light sauce is obtained. Strain, then mix in the butter, shaking the pan until it has blended in.

4 Cook the carrot, celery and leek in salted boiling water for 3–4 minutes. Drain, pour on cold water to stop the cooking, then drain again and add all the vegetables and seafood, including the prawns, to the sauce to heat through. Mix in some of the lemon rind and check the seasoning, adding more rind to taste.

5 Serve the soup sprinkled with chervil or parsley.

Chef's tip Julienne strips are even-sized strips of vegetables the size and shape of matchsticks.

Cream of cauliflower soup

In France, this soup is known as Potage à la du Barry. It is named after a mistress of Louis XV of France, Comtesse du Barry, whose name is given to a number of dishes that contain cauliflower.

Preparation time **25 minutes**
Total cooking time **35 minutes**
Serves 4

300 g (10 oz) cauliflower, chopped
15 g (¹/2 oz) unsalted butter
I small onion, finely chopped
I small leek, white part only, finely sliced
15 g (¹/2 oz) plain flour
750 ml (24 fl oz) milk

GARNISH
90 g (3 oz) small cauliflower florets
100 g (3¹/4 oz) clarified butter (see page 63)
or 100 ml (3¹/4 fl oz) oil
4 slices bread, cut into cubes
50 ml (1³/4 fl oz) cream, for whipping
chopped fresh chervil, to garnish

1 Place the cauliflower in a large pan, pour on 100 ml (3¹/4 fl oz) water. If the cauliflower is not completely covered by the water, add some milk to cover. Bring to the boil, turn the heat down and simmer for 7 minutes, or until soft. Purée the cauliflower and cooking liquid together in a blender or food processor until smooth.

2 In a medium pan, melt the butter over low heat. Add the onion and leek, press on a buttered piece of greaseproof paper or a lid and cook for 5 minutes, or until soft but not coloured. Add the flour and cook for at least 1 minute, stirring continuously, until pale blonde in colour. Remove from the heat, stir in the milk until the mixture is smooth, then return to the heat and bring to the boil, stirring continuously. Add the purée of cauliflower to the pan and season to taste. Remove from the heat, cover and keep to one side.

3 To make the garnish, bring a small saucepan of salted water to the boil and cook the cauliflower florets for about 2 minutes, then refresh in cold water. Drain well in a colander or sieve and set aside.

4 Heat a frying pan with the clarified butter or oil over high heat. Add the bread cubes and fry, stirring gently, until golden brown. Remove, drain on crumpled paper towels and salt while warm to keep them crisp.

5 Reheat the soup, season with salt and freshly ground black pepper and pour into bowls. Use the cream to thin the soup if it is too thick. Alternatively, lightly whip the cream and then stir into the soup so that the swirls show as streaks through it. Sprinkle with the cauliflower florets, chervil and croutons.

Minestrone

This is a traditional version of the Italian classic. The soup can be thickened with either white beans or perhaps spaghetti, and a generous spoonful of Parmesan added at the table.

Preparation time 20 minutes + soaking overnight
Total cooking time 1 hour 30 minutes
Serves 6

40 g (1¼ oz) white beans (haricot or navy beans)
1.5 litres chicken stock (see page 62)
35 g (1¼ oz) unsalted butter
1 onion, sliced
2 carrots, finely chopped
2 celery sticks, sliced
2 leeks, white part only, thinly sliced
1 tablespoon tomato paste
2 rashers smoked bacon, cut into cubes
2 cloves garlic, crushed
bouquet garni (see page 63)
250 g (8 oz) green cabbage, roughly shredded
50 g (1¾ oz) green peas
100 g (3¼ oz) Parmesan, freshly grated

1 Place the dried beans in a bowl, cover with twice their volume of cold water, then leave to soak overnight. Drain, then rinse the soaked beans under cold running water. Heat the chicken stock in a large pan, add the drained beans and bring slowly to the boil over medium heat. Cook for 45 minutes, or until the beans are tender, skimming the surface often.

2 Melt the butter in a large saucepan over low heat. Add the onion, carrot, celery and leek and cook gently for 10 minutes, or until soft but not coloured. Add the tomato paste to the pan, mix in and cook for 1–2 minutes, stirring continuously to prevent burning. Add the bacon, garlic and bouquet garni.

3 Pour the beans and their stock over the tomato mixture and stir until well combined. Season to taste with salt and pepper. Simmer the soup for 20 minutes, add the cabbage and cook until soft, then toss in the peas and cook for an additional 5 minutes. Remove the bouquet garni and season the soup to taste.

4 Ladle the soup into bowls. Serve with the grated Parmesan on the side.

Chef's tip This soup should be thick with vegetables and beans, but do make sure that it has enough liquid to still eat as a soup. Add more water, if necessary, while the soup simmers.

Cream of tomato soup

This soup is best made with fresh tomatoes that are in season and very ripe. The result is a soup with that beautifully sweet tomato flavour.

Preparation time **15 minutes**
Total cooking time **35 minutes**
Serves **6**

1 1/2 tablespoons olive oil
I onion, sliced
2 cloves garlic, chopped
3 large stalks of fresh basil
I sprig of fresh thyme
I bay leaf
2 tablespoons tomato paste
I kg (2 lb) very ripe tomatoes, quartered
pinch of sugar
250 ml (8 fl oz) chicken stock (see page 62)
100 ml (3 1/4 fl oz) cream
fresh basil leaves, cut into fine strips, to garnish

1 Heat a pan with the oil and gently cook the onion for 3 minutes, or until it is soft without being coloured.
2 Add the garlic, basil stalks, thyme, bay leaf, tomato paste and the fresh tomatoes. Season with the sugar, salt and black pepper. Pour in the chicken stock and bring to the boil, reduce the heat, cover and simmer for about 15 minutes. Discard the bay leaf.
3 Purée in a blender or food processor and strain through a fine sieve. Return to the pan, stir in the cream and reheat. Check the seasoning.
4 Serve the soup in bowls or one large soup dish, garnishing the top with strips of basil.

Chef's tip If tomatoes are out of season and lack flavour, the same quantity of canned tomatoes can be used and will also give excellent results.

Mussel soup

This is a delicious and delicate mussel velouté soup, lightly flavoured with saffron and cooked in a sauce of white wine and fish stock.

*Preparation time **35 minutes + 10 minutes soaking***
*Total cooking time **30 minutes***
Serves 4

1.25 kg (2 lb 8 oz) mussels
50 g (1³/4 oz) unsalted butter
1 celery stick, finely chopped
4 French shallots, thinly sliced
30 g (1 oz) fresh parsley, chopped
300 ml (10 fl oz) dry white wine
300 ml (10 fl oz) fish stock (see page 62)
350 ml (11¹/4 fl oz) cream
2 large pinches of saffron threads
20 g (³/4 oz) plain flour
40 g (1¹/4 oz) chilled unsalted butter, cut into cubes
2 egg yolks
fresh chervil leaves, to garnish

1 Scrub the mussels well. Using a blunt knife, scrape off any barnacles and trim away the hairy beard on the straight side. Discard any mussels that remain open when tapped gently on a work surface.

2 Melt 30 g (1 oz) of butter in a large saucepan and gently cook the celery and shallots until soft but not brown. Add the mussels, parsley and wine. Cover and simmer for 4 minutes, or until the mussels have opened. Take the musssels out of the pan and reserve the cooking liquid. Throw away any that have not opened and remove the mussels from the shells of those that have opened.

3 Strain the reserved liquid and simmer to reduce by half. Add the fish stock and 300 ml (10 fl oz) of the cream and simmer. Add the saffron and black pepper, to taste. Combine the remaining 20 g (³/4 oz) of butter and the flour together in a bowl and whisk into the soup. Simmer the soup to cook the flour and then add the chilled butter, shaking the pan until it has blended in.

4 In a bowl, mix the egg yolks and the rest of the cream together, pour in a little hot soup and then add to the pan. Do not allow it to boil, simply warm the soup or the yolks will cook to small scrambled pieces.

5 Add the mussels to the soup to heat them through. Serve garnished with some fresh chervil leaves.

Chef's tip The mussels must be alive when cooked. They deteriorate quickly and if, before cooking, they remain open, they are dead and should not be used.

Scotch broth

This warming Scottish soup is sometimes served as two courses, the unstrained broth followed by the tender meat. Traditionally made with mutton, it is now more often made with lamb.

Preparation time **30 minutes + 1–2 hours soaking**
Total cooking time **1 hour 30 minutes**
Serves 4

30 g (1 oz) barley
400 g (12³⁄₄ oz) lamb neck or mutton, boned
  (ask your butcher to do this)
30 g (1 oz) unsalted butter
1 small carrot, finely diced
¹⁄₂ small turnip, finely diced
1 small leek, finely diced
¹⁄₂ small onion, finely diced
60 g (2 oz) frozen green peas
30 g (1 oz) fresh parsley, chopped

1 Place the barley in a bowl, cover well with cold water and allow to soak for 1–2 hours. Drain the barley and rinse under cold running water. Bring a pan of water to the boil, add the barley and cook for 15 minutes, or until tender. Drain the barley and set aside.

2 Trim any excess fat from the meat then cut the meat into small cubes. Half fill a medium pan with salted water and bring to the boil. Add the lamb and cook for 2 minutes, then drain and plunge the lamb into a bowl of cold water. This process will give clarity to the soup and further remove traces of fat. Rinse the pan, half fill with salted water once more and bring to the boil. Add the meat, reduce the heat and simmer for 30–40 minutes, or until the meat is tender. Strain, reserving the meat, and measure the cooking liquid to 1 litre, adding extra water if necessary.

3 Place the butter in a large saucepan and melt over medium heat. Add the diced vegetables to the pan and cook, stirring frequently, until tender but not coloured. Drain the vegetables and wipe out the pan with paper towels. Replace the vegetables then mix in the lamb, barley and peas. Add the stock and bring to the boil. Reduce the heat and simmer for 30 minutes, while frequently skimming the surface to remove excess fat and impurities. Season to taste and serve the soup with a sprinkling of parsley to garnish.

Celeriac and Stilton soup

Celeriac tastes like a sweeter and more nutty version of celery, and is partnered here by Stilton, the king of English cheeses.

Preparation time **5 minutes**
Total cooking time **40 minutes**
Serves 4

1¹/2 tablespoons oil or 30 g (1 oz) unsalted butter
1 onion, sliced
200 g (6¹/2 oz) celeriac, peeled and thinly sliced
100 g (3¹/4 oz) Stilton cheese, crumbled
fresh watercress, to garnish

1 In a large pan, heat the oil or butter and add the onion. Cover the pan and cook over low heat until the onion is translucent. Add the celeriac and 1 litre water, cover and bring to the boil. Reduce the heat and simmer for 30 minutes, or until the celeriac is very soft.

2 Add 75 g (2¹/2 oz) of the Stilton and purée the mixture in a blender or food processor. Return the soup to a clean pan and reheat gently. Season with salt and freshly ground black pepper to taste, bearing in mind that Stilton can be very salty.

3 Serve with the remaining cheese crumbled over the surface. Garnish with a few sprigs of watercress and some freshly ground black pepper.

Chef's tip Celeriac discolours when it is peeled, so if preparing in advance, place in a bowl, cover with water and add a tablespoon of lemon juice.

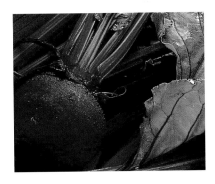

Borscht

This vegetarian Borscht is based on a recipe from the Ukraine, where Borscht is the national soup. It is characterised by its thickness and the deep red colour of its main ingredient—beetroot.

Preparation time **40 minutes**
Total cooking time **45 minutes**
Serves 6

3 litres water
I tablespoon tomato paste
500 g (I lb) fresh beetroot, cut into julienne strips (see Chef's tip)
I carrot, cut into julienne strips
125 g (4 oz) parsnips, cut into julienne strips
4 celery sticks, cut into julienne strips
I onion, finely chopped
2 cloves garlic
350 g (11 1/4 oz) cabbage, coarsely shredded
6 ripe tomatoes
30 g (I oz) fresh parsley, finely chopped
60 g (2 oz) plain flour
125 ml (4 fl oz) sour cream

1 Bring the 3 litres of water to the boil in a large saucepan and season with salt and freshly ground black pepper. Stir the tomato paste into the liquid with the beetroot, carrot, parsnip and celery and simmer for about 15 minutes. Add the onion, garlic and shredded cabbage and continue to simmer the soup for an additional 15 minutes.

2 Cut a small cross in the base of each tomato and place in boiling water for 10 seconds, then immediately immerse them in cold water. Peel, quarter, seed and roughly chop them.

3 Check the soup for seasoning and add the tomato. Simmer for 5 minutes and stir through the parsley. Thicken the soup by mixing the flour into the sour cream, then stirring it into the soup over low heat until well combined.

4 Adjust the flavour of the soup with some salt and a little sugar if necessary. The borscht should be slightly piquant, but not sweet. The flavour is improved if the soup is made a day in advance and then reheated just before serving.

Chef's tip Julienne strips are evenly sized vegetable strips, the size and shape of matchsticks.

Prawn bisque

The original bisque was a crayfish purée, thickened with bread. Today, all kinds of shellfish are used and the soup is usually finished with fresh cream. The result is a rich and elegant soup.

*Preparation time **35 minutes***
*Total cooking time **1 hour***
Serves 6

600 g (1¼ lb) small cooked prawns, shells on
30 g (1 oz) unsalted butter, for cooking
1 small carrot, chopped
½ small onion, chopped
1 celery stick, chopped
½ leek, chopped
1 tablespoon brandy
1 tablespoon tomato paste
2 ripe tomatoes, cut into quarters
3 fresh tarragon sprigs
bouquet garni (see page 63)
150 ml (5 fl oz) white wine
350 ml (11¼ fl oz) fish stock (see page 62)
300 ml (10 fl oz) cream
small pinch of cayenne pepper
40 g (1¼ oz) chilled unsalted butter, cut into cubes
1 teaspoon rice flour (optional)
fresh chopped dill, to garnish

1 Reserve 18 whole prawns for decoration. Roughly chop the remainder with the shells.

2 Heat the butter in a large pan and add the carrot, onion, celery and leek. Cover and cook over low heat until the vegetables are soft, but not coloured. Add the chopped prawns and their shells and cook gently for about 5 minutes. Add the brandy and boil, scraping the base of the pan to pick up any sticky juices, then allow the liquid to evaporate. Add the tomato paste, tomato and tarragon sprigs and cook for about 30 seconds, stirring continuously, then add the bouquet garni. Pour in the white wine and allow it to evaporate to a syrup before adding the fish stock and the cream. Bring to the boil, reduce the heat, cover and simmer gently for 15–18 minutes.

3 Mix vigorously and then strain through a fine sieve. Check the seasoning, adding salt and cayenne pepper if desired. Mix in the chilled butter, shaking the pan until it has blended in. The soup will thicken as the liquid takes in the butter to form an emulsion.

4 If the bisque is not thick enough, mix the rice flour with a little water and then gradually whisk this mixture into the hot bisque until the desired consistency has been achieved. If it is too thick, dilute with a little more fish stock.

5 Divide the reserved whole prawns among six bowls. Pour the soup over them and garnish with a little chopped dill.

Creamy garlic soup with black olive crostini

*This unusual soup has its roots in the garlic-based soups of the Mediterranean. The black olive crostini
would also go beautifully with many of the other cream soups in this book.*

*Preparation time **20 minutes***
*Total cooking time **45 minutes***
Serves 4

90 g (3 oz) unsalted butter
2 heads of garlic, peeled into individual cloves
2 onions, finely chopped
300 g (10 oz) floury potatoes, cut into cubes
500 ml (16 fl oz) milk
500 ml (16 fl oz) chicken stock (see page 62) or water

BLACK OLIVE CROSTINI
4 slices of French baguette
100 g (3 1/4 oz) black olives, pitted and finely chopped
50 ml (1 3/4 fl oz) olive oil

1 Melt 30 g (1 oz) of the butter in a medium saucepan over medium heat. Add the garlic cloves and cook for 5–7 minutes, or until golden in colour. Add the onion, cook gently for 2–3 minutes, then add the potato and the remaining 60 g (2 oz) of butter and continue to cook for 7–10 minutes, or until the onions begin to soften. Stir frequently as the starchy potatoes will want to stick to the pan. Pour in the milk and stock or water, then cook gently for 15 minutes, or until the potatoes are very soft.

2 Purée the soup in batches in a food processor or blender. Return to the rinsed pan and season to taste with salt and freshly ground black pepper. Cover to keep warm and set aside.

3 To make the black olive crostini, toast the four round slices of French baguette under the grill until golden brown on both sides. Place the finely chopped olives in a small bowl and moisten with the oil to lightly bind. Season to taste with salt and freshly ground black pepper and spread onto the crostini.

4 Ladle the soup into bowls and serve with the crostini.

Thai hot and sour prawn soup

This famous soup is known in Thailand as Tom Yum Goong and acts as a piquant balance to the rich coconut flavour of Thai curries. If you want the soup a little less hot, lessen the chillies.

Preparation time **30 minutes**
Total cooking time **20 minutes**
Serves 4

500 g (1 lb) large raw prawns, shells on
2 tablespoons vegetable oil
2–3 stalks lemon grass, white part only, cut into 2 cm (3/4 inch) pieces and bruised with the side of a knife
1 tablespoon chopped or grated fresh ginger
3 cloves garlic
2 tablespoons coriander stalks, roughly chopped
4 black peppercorns
2 small red chillies
2 small green chillies
4 lime leaves, shredded
2 spring onions, sliced
1 1/2 tablespoons fish sauce (nam pla)
1 1/2 tablespoons lime juice
fresh coriander leaves, to garnish

1 Peel and devein the prawns, keeping the tails intact and reserving the heads and shells. Cover and refrigerate the prawns. Rinse the heads and shells and dry well.

2 Heat the vegetable oil in a wide, shallow pan or wok, then add the prawn shells and heads, lemon grass stalks and ginger and stir-fry over high heat for 3–4 minutes. Add 1.5 litres water and bring to the boil, skimming the surface continuously. Reduce the heat, cover the pan and simmer for about 10 minutes. Strain the soup through a fine sieve and discard the prawn shells, heads and seasonings. Pour the liquid into a clean saucepan and set aside.

3 With a mortar and pestle, or in a small bowl using the end of a rolling pin, mix the garlic, coriander stalks and peppercorns to a smooth paste.

4 Split down the length of the chillies, remove the seeds and cut into thin slices. You may want to wear rubber gloves as these chillies are very hot and can cause a strong burning sensation.

5 Return the stock to the boil and add the combined garlic, coriander and peppercorns with the lime leaves, spring onion and prawns. Simmer for 3–4 minutes, or until the prawns become pink and opaque. Remove from the heat and add the red and green chilli, fish sauce and lime juice. Taste to check the seasoning. You may want to add a little more lime juice or fish sauce. Garnish with the coriander leaves and serve.

Cream of mushroom soup

This soup combines wild and cultivated mushrooms to create a rich, complex flavour. Try using some of the new varieties becoming more widely available to create different flavours.

Preparation time **20 minutes**
Total cooking time **30 minutes**

Serves 6

200 g (6¹/2 oz) wild mushrooms, such as chanterelles or cèpes
300 g (10 oz) button mushrooms
30 g (1 oz) unsalted butter
4 French shallots, finely chopped
500 ml (16 fl oz) chicken stock (see page 62)
300 ml (10 fl oz) cream
5–6 sprigs of fresh chervil
30 g (1 oz) chilled unsalted butter, cut into cubes
60 ml (2 fl oz) cream, for whipping

1 Place the wild mushrooms in a sieve and shake off some of the sand and dirt. Thoroughly clean by tossing them in a large bowl full of water, but do not leave them in the water too long as they will absorb too much liquid. Lift them out and finely slice. Clean the button mushrooms by wiping with paper towels.

2 Melt the butter in a medium pan. Add the shallots and cook over low heat, covered, for 1–2 minutes. Add the mushrooms, cover and cook for 2–3 minutes. Pour the chicken stock and the cream into the pan and season with salt and pepper. Add three or four chervil sprigs and simmer for 12–15 minutes.

3 Pour the soup into a blender or food processor and purée. Sieve the purée into a clean saucepan, heat gently and toss in the chilled butter, shaking the pan until it has blended in. Season to taste with salt and freshly ground black pepper.

4 In a bowl, beat the cream to soft peaks and season with a little salt and pepper.

5 Pour the soup into bowls. Using two dessertspoons, form neat, oval quenelle-like shapes from the whipped cream and place one on top of the soup in each bowl. Decorate with the remaining chervil.

Chef's tip If the wild mushrooms are only available as dried, use half the weight and then soak overnight in enough cold water to just cover them. The resulting soaking liquid has a strong flavour and is an excellent substitute for all or some of the chicken stock in this recipe, or can be added to stews or casseroles.

Smoked salmon soup with lime Chantilly cream

If at Christmas, or another special occasion, you order a smoked salmon as a whole side with skin and bones, don't throw the trimmings away. Keep them in the freezer to make this elegant soup.

Preparation time **30 minutes**
Total cooking time **1 hour**
Serves 8

30 g (1 oz) unsalted butter
1 onion, finely chopped
3 French shallots, finely chopped
1/2 fennel bulb, finely chopped
1 celery stick, finely chopped
1 leek, finely chopped
1 carrot, finely chopped
750 g (1 1/2 lb) smoked salmon trimmings
375 ml (12 fl oz) white wine
bouquet garni (see page 63)
10 white peppercorns
1 star anise
1 tablespoon mixed fresh herbs, such as parsley, chervil
1.8 litres fish stock (see page 62) or water
150 ml (5 fl oz) thick (double) cream
chopped fresh chives, to garnish
50 g (1 3/4 oz) smoked salmon, to garnish

LIME CHANTILLY CREAM
150 ml (5 fl oz) cream, for whipping
finely grated rind of 1 lime

1 Melt the butter in a large frying pan over medium heat and add the onion, shallots, fennel, celery, leek and carrot and cook, stirring continuously, for 10 minutes, or until soft but not coloured. Remove half the vegetables from the pan and set aside.

2 Add the salmon to the vegetables in the pan and cook gently for 2 minutes, without colouring. Add the wine, bouquet garni, peppercorns, star anise and mixed herbs and season with salt and freshly ground black pepper. Bring to the boil, reduce the liquid by half, then add the fish stock. Reduce the heat and simmer for 25 minutes, skimming the surface frequently, then strain through a sieve and discard the salmon trimmings, vegetables and seasonings.

3 Transfer the liquid to a clean pan, add the reserved vegetables and cook for 10 minutes over medium heat. Strain once more, discarding the vegetables, return the soup to the pan and stir in the cream. Season to taste with salt and pepper, then set aside and keep warm.

4 To make the lime Chantilly cream, lightly whisk the cream in a small bowl to softly hold its shape, add the grated lime rind and gently fold in.

5 Serve the soup hot or cold with the chopped chives sprinkled on top. Add a spoonful of lime Chantilly cream in the centre and top with a small roll of thinly sliced salmon.

Cream of vegetable soup

You can use different vegetables for this soup depending on the season. This is a thick, winter version, but a spring vegetable soup is also delicious.

*Preparation time **15 minutes***
*Total cooking time **1 hour***
Serves 6

100 g (3¹/4 oz) unsalted butter
300 g (10 oz) potatoes, cut into cubes
1 carrot, cut into cubes
¹/2 onion, cut into cubes
2 small leeks, white part only, thinly sliced
1 celery stick, thinly sliced
bouquet garni (see page 63)
200 ml (6¹/2 fl oz) cream
chopped fresh chervil or parsley, to garnish

1 Heat the butter in a saucepan, add the vegetables, cover, and cook over a low heat until soft. Add the bouquet garni. Pour on 1.5 litres water, bring to the boil, reduce the heat and simmer for 30 minutes. Lift out and discard the bouquet garni.
2 Purée the soup, in batches, in a blender or food processor, then sieve into a clean pan and cook over low heat for 10 minutes.
3 Add the cream and season to taste with salt and pepper. Serve very hot sprinkled with the chervil or parsley and accompanied by crusty bread.

Singapore laksa

Traditionally, fresh soft laksa noodles are used for this wonderfully spicy and creamy soup. If you can't find them, then the thin Chinese noodles used below make a good alternative.

Preparation time **25 minutes**
Total cooking time **35 minutes**
Serves **4**

18 medium cooked prawns, shells on
4 Asian shallots, chopped
3 cloves garlic, chopped
5 dried chillies, chopped
2 stalks lemon grass, white part only, sliced
3 teaspoons ground turmeric
1 tablespoon shrimp paste
1/2 teaspoon ground coriander
1 litre coconut milk
2 tablespoons oil
2 tablespoons sugar
500 g (1 lb) skinless chicken breast fillets
250 ml (8 fl oz) chicken stock (see page 62)
250 g (8 oz) dried fine Chinese egg noodles
whole or sliced fresh mint leaves, to garnish
1 spring onion, sliced, to garnish
1 red chilli, seeded and thinly sliced, to garnish

1 Peel and devein the prawns. Cover and place in the refrigerator until ready to use.

2 Process the shallots and garlic in a blender or food processor to a smooth pulp. Add the dried chillies, lemon grass, turmeric, shrimp paste, coriander and 60 ml (2 fl oz) of the coconut milk. Process all the ingredients to a smooth paste.

3 Heat the oil in a medium saucepan, add the paste and fry for 1 minute, stirring continuously, until fragrant. Add 300 ml (10 fl oz) water, the remaining coconut milk, sugar and 1 teaspoon salt and stir until the mixture just boils. Lower the heat and simmer gently for 10 minutes.

4 Poach the chicken by placing in a small pan and pouring over enough of the chicken stock to cover. Simmer for 8 minutes, covered, until cooked through, then cut into cubes.

5 Meanwhile, bring a large pan of salted water to the boil. Crush the noodles lightly with your fingers, add to the pan and simmer for 7 minutes, or until the noodles are *al dente*. Drain and rinse in warm water to remove the excess starch and prevent them from sticking together, but not to cool them completely.

6 Divide the noodles, prawns and pieces of chicken between four bowls and pour the hot soup over. Arrange the mint leaves and slices of spring onion and red chilli on top and serve immediately.

Minted green pea soup with croutons

Mint and green peas are a classic culinary partnership, here puréed together into a deliciously fragrant soup with a fairly light consistency.

*Preparation time **25 minutes***
*Total cooking time **40 minutes***
Serves 4

1 small butter or round lettuce, roughly sliced
12 spring onions or 1 small onion, sliced
450 g (14¼ oz) frozen baby peas, thawed
1–2 sprigs of fresh mint
1.2 litres chicken stock (see page 62)
4 slices bread
oil, for cooking
30 g (1 oz) unsalted butter
30 g (1 oz) plain flour
150 ml (5 fl oz) cream

1 Put the lettuce, spring onion or onion and peas into a large saucepan with the mint. Pour on the chicken stock and bring to the boil. Then reduce the heat and simmer for 25 minutes. Purée the soup in batches in a blender or food processor, then pass through a fine sieve.

2 Meanwhile, remove the crusts from the bread and cut into small cubes. Heat the oil and fry the cubes until lightly browned, stirring with a spoon to colour evenly. Lift out and drain on crumpled paper towels and salt lightly while hot. This will season them, but also helps to keep them crisp.

3 Melt the butter in a large pan over medium heat, stir in the flour and cook for 1 minute. Do not allow to brown. Remove from the heat, add the puréed soup and mix well. Return to the stove on low to medium heat and bring slowly to the boil, stirring continuously. Add the cream and season with salt and pepper. Serve in bowls with the croutons sprinkled in first.

Chef's tip You may consider the cream optional if you wish, or lightly whisk and serve either swirled through the soup or as a spoonful on top. To vary the garnish, cook 30 g (1 oz) extra of baby peas and use to replace the croutons.

Fish soup

French cuisine has a number of wonderful traditional fish soups, making good use of fresh fish simmered with herbs and wine. This is a light soup, but with a surprising depth of flavour.

Preparation time **30 minutes**
Total cooking time **1 hour**
Serves 6

1 John Dory, about 400 g (12³/4 oz), filleted
4 red mullet, about 600 g (1¹/4 lb), filleted
2 red gurnard or coral trout, about 400 g (12³/4 oz), filleted
500 g (1 lb) conger eel or blue grenadier, filleted (see Chef's tips)
50 ml (1³/4 fl oz) olive oil
1 small carrot, finely chopped
¹/2 small onion, finely chopped
¹/2 leek, cut into 2 cm (³/4 inch) cubes
3 cloves garlic, chopped
2 sprigs of thyme
1 bay leaf
1 tablespoon tomato paste
80 g (2³/4 oz) fresh parsley, chopped
4 tomatoes, quartered and seeds removed
200 ml (6¹/2 fl oz) white wine
3 tablespoons Cognac
200 ml (6¹/2 fl oz) cream
2 large pinches of cayenne pepper
2 large pinches of saffron threads

1 Wash the fish fillets and conger eel thoroughly under plenty of water. Pat dry with paper towels and cut into 3–5 cm (1¹/4–2 inch) cubes. Cover and refrigerate until ready to use.

2 Heat the olive oil in a pan, add the carrot, onion, leek and garlic and cook over low heat for 5 minutes. Add the thyme sprigs, bay leaf and the tomato paste. Mix well for 5 minutes. Stir in the pieces of fish and cook for another 5 minutes. Add 2 litres water, the chopped parsley and tomato and simmer for about 30 minutes. Pour in the white wine and Cognac and stir over low heat for about 2 minutes.

3 Pour the mixture through a fine sieve and press very hard to take all the flavours and juices of the ingredients into the resulting liquid. Discard the fish pieces, vegetables and herbs. Pour the liquid into a clean pan and heat gently over low heat. Add the cream, cayenne pepper, saffron threads and season to taste with salt and freshly ground black pepper. Cook gently for about 5 minutes. Serve the soup sprinkled with freshly ground black pepper.

Chef's tips Ask your fishmonger to scale, gut, head and fillet the fish and to skin and clean the eel.

If one kind of fish is not available, you can increase the amount of one of the others.

Cream of asparagus soup

Asparagus is one of the most delicious of the spring vegetables. In this simple soup, which can be served hot or cold, the flavour of the asparagus comes to the fore.

*Preparation time **15 minutes***
*Total cooking time **20 minutes***
Serves 4

800 g (1 lb 10 oz) green or white asparagus
500 ml (16 fl oz) chicken stock (see page 62)
265 ml (8¹/2 fl oz) cream or thick (double) cream
pinch of sugar
1 tablespoon cornflour or potato flour
1–2 tablespoons water or milk
2 tablespoons chopped fresh chervil, to garnish

1 Peel and discard the tough skin from the base of the asparagus and trim the thick ends. Wash and drain. Cut off the tips 3 cm (1¹/4 inches) down the asparagus and set aside. Slice the stalks into thin rounds. Bring a pan of salted water to the boil, add the asparagus tips and simmer briefly for about 2 minutes. Drain and place in a bowl of iced water to stop them from cooking further.

2 Add the chicken stock and 250 ml (8 fl oz) of cream to a large pan with the sugar and some salt and pepper and bring to the boil. Add the sliced asparagus and cook gently for 10 minutes.

3 Purée in a food processor or blender, then pass through a fine sieve. Return the mixture to a clean pan and heat again. In a small bowl, mix the cornflour or potato flour with the water or milk until it forms a smooth paste. Pour a little hot asparagus mixture into the paste. Blend, return to the pan, and bring to the boil, stirring continuously. This procedure ensures a lump-free result when using a dry, starchy powder to thicken a hot liquid. Season to taste with salt and freshly ground black pepper.

4 Pour the soup into a dish or bowls. Swirl the remaining 15 ml (¹/2 fl oz) of cream in the centre, arrange some asparagus tips on top and sprinkle with the chopped chervil.

Gazpacho

This famous Spanish soup is traditionally made in a large clay bowl with ripe, bright red tomatoes. It should be served ice cold.

Preparation time **35 minutes + 2 hours refrigeration**
Total cooking time **Nil**
Serves 6–8

75 g (2¹/₂ oz) fresh white bread, crusts removed
30 ml (1 fl oz) red wine vinegar
2 cloves garlic
1³/₄ telegraph cucumbers, unpeeled and roughly chopped
1 onion, chopped
¹/₂ green capsicum (pepper), roughly chopped
1.75 kg (3¹/₂ lb) tomatoes, quartered and seeded
125 ml (4 fl oz) olive oil

GARNISH
¹/₄ telegraph cucumber, unpeeled
¹/₂ green capsicum (pepper)
4 slices of bread, crusts removed and toasted

1 In a food processor or blender, process the bread into fine breadcrumbs and add the vinegar, garlic, cucumber, onion, capsicum, tomato and a teaspoon of salt. Purée and then push through a sieve.

2 Return to the food processor or blender and pour in the olive oil in a thin steady stream. Alternatively, pour the mixture into a large bowl and briskly stir or whisk in the oil.

3 Taste and season with salt and freshly ground black pepper. A little more vinegar may be required for a refreshing tang. Check the consistency, it should be thinnish, so you may need to dilute with a little water. Cover with double plastic wrap and chill in the refrigerator for at least 2 hours.

4 To make the garnish, halve the remaining cucumber lengthways and use the point of a teaspoon to scoop out the seeds. Cut the cucumber, capsicum and bread into small cubes.

5 Pour the soup into well-chilled bowls and pass round the cucumber, capsicum and croutons in separate dishes for each person to sprinkle onto their own soup.

Chef's tips To serve, you could add two or three ice cubes to chill the soup, or for more colour, chop a red capsicum with the green.

Make the soup a day in advance for a mature, well-rounded flavour, but cover well, the soup has a strong smell that can affect other foods in the refrigerator.

Cream of chicken soup

This soup is quick and easy to prepare. It is based on a simple stock made from chicken wings, which can be ready in just 30 minutes. You could also use the more traditional stock from the Chef's techniques.

Preparation time **10 minutes**
Total cooking time **50 minutes**
Serves 6

1 leek, roughly chopped
1 small carrot, roughly chopped
1 small onion, roughly chopped
1 celery stick, roughly chopped
400 g (12³/4 oz) chicken wings
2 sprigs of fresh tarragon
bouquet garni (see page 63)
6 black peppercorns
1 clove
35 g (1¹/4 oz) unsalted butter
35 g (1¹/4 oz) plain flour
250 ml (8 fl oz) cream
1 skinless chicken breast fillet
a few fresh tarragon sprigs, to garnish
2 egg yolks

1 Add the leek, carrot, onion, celery, chicken wings, tarragon, bouquet garni, peppercorns and clove to a large saucepan. Pour in 1.5 litres water to cover and bring to the boil, then turn down the heat and simmer for 30–35 minutes. Skim frequently for a clear finish.

2 Pour the stock through a colander and measure about 1 litre of the liquid, reserving the rest. In a medium pan, melt the butter, add the flour and cook gently, stirring continuously, for 1 minute, or until a smooth paste is formed and the flour is cooked. Remove from the heat. Pour the 1 litre of hot stock into the cooled butter and flour mixture a little at a time and stir well between each addition. Return the pan to the heat and continue to stir until the mixture boils and thickens. Add 200 ml (6¹/2 fl oz) of the cream and return to the boil. Season to taste with salt and pepper.

3 Cook the chicken breast for 8 minutes in enough of the reserved stock to just cover it. Drain and cut into small cubes. Remove the leaves from the remaining tarragon stems and place in boiling salted water, cook for 30 seconds then drain. Mix the egg yolks with the rest of the cream and add to the soup. Do not boil the mixture any further. Add the chicken cubes and sprinkle over some tarragon leaves and some freshly ground black pepper to garnish.

Vegetable and saffron consommé

*This beautifully light consommé is very low in fat and excellent
for getting you in shape.*

*Preparation time **30 minutes***
*Total cooking time **1 hour 5 minutes***
Serves 6

VEGETABLE STOCK
1 onion, roughly chopped
1 carrot, roughly chopped
1 celery stick, roughly chopped
1/2 fennel bulb, roughly chopped
1 leek, roughly chopped
80 g (2³/4 oz) button mushrooms, chopped
2 ripe tomatoes, quartered, seeded and chopped
2 cloves garlic, halved
6 white peppercorns
small pinch of ground nutmeg
1 tablespoon finely grated orange rind
bouquet garni (see page 63)

2 large pinches of saffron threads
1 ripe tomato
1/2 small leek, cut into julienne strips (see Chef's tip)
1/2 small carrot, cut into julienne strips
1/2 stick celery, cut into julienne strips
6 quail eggs
chopped fresh chives and chervil, to garnish

1 To make the vegetable stock, add the vegetables to a large saucepan and pour over 1.5 litres water. Mix in the garlic, peppercorns, nutmeg, orange rind, bouquet garni and a large pinch of salt. Bring to the boil, cover and reduce the heat to simmer gently for 45 minutes.

2 Strain through a wire sieve and discard the vegetables and flavourings. Measure out 1 litre of the stock, making up the volume with water if necessary, and pour into a large, clean pan. Add the saffron and set aside.

3 Cut a cross in the skin at the base of the tomato. Plunge into boiling water for 10 seconds, then put into iced water. Peel, and then with the point of a knife, remove the stem. Quarter the tomato, remove the seeds, then finely dice the flesh.

4 Add the leek, carrot and celery to a pan of boiling salted water. Cook for 5 minutes, or until tender, and drain. Add these to the measured stock with the tomato cubes and season to taste, then reheat without boiling.

5 Bring a small pan of salted water to the boil. Gently lower in the quail eggs and simmer for 3–4 minutes. Remove the shells and place in a soup dish. Pour over the hot consommé and sprinkle with the chopped chives and chervil.

Chef's tip Julienne strips are evenly sized vegetable strips, the size and shape of matchsticks.

Chicken, bacon and lentil soup

Lentils are excellent for thickening winter soups and are here partnered with chicken and the traditional bacon. Brown and green lentils have the best texture for soups, but yellow and red lentils can also be used.

Preparation time **40 minutes + overnight soaking**
Total cooking time **1 hour 40 minutes**
Serves 4

300 g (10 oz) brown or green lentils
1 chicken, weighing 1.8 kg (3lb 10 oz)
50 g (1³/4 oz) unsalted butter
100 g (3¹/4 oz) bacon, cut into cubes
1 carrot, sliced
1 small onion, sliced
1 celery stick, sliced
bouquet garni (see page 63)
few sprigs of fresh flat-leaf parsley, to garnish

1 Soak the lentils in cold water overnight. Rinse and drain well.

2 Remove the skin from the chicken. Then remove the breast meat and set aside. Chop up the legs, wings and the carcass. In a large stockpot, melt the butter and add the bacon and chicken legs, wings and carcass and brown over medium heat for 7–10 minutes. When nicely coloured, add the vegetables, bouquet garni, 3 litres cold water and the lentils. Place back on the heat and allow to simmer for 1 hour, occasionally skimming the foam off the top.

3 Meanwhile, season the chicken breasts with salt and pepper and pan-fry over medium heat for 5 minutes on each side, or until cooked to a golden-brown. Set aside to cool.

4 Take the chicken pieces out of the stockpot with tongs and remove the meat, discarding the bones. Place the chicken meat back in the stockpot and simmer for about 15 minutes. Remove the bouquet garni, then purée the soup in a blender or food processor. Return to a clean pan over low heat and season with salt and freshly ground black pepper to taste.

5 Cut the cooled chicken breasts into small cubes and add to the soup to heat through. Serve garnished with a few sprigs of parsley.

Chef's tip If you want to enrich the flavour of this soup, a few spoons of cream and butter can be mixed in just before serving.

New England clam chowder

Clams are very popular on the east coast of the United States, where they are caught in the coastal waters and eaten raw or cooked the same day. Make sure the clams you use for this chowder are very fresh.

*Preparation time **40 minutes + 30 minutes soaking***
*Total cooking time **1 hour 15 minutes***
Serves 4

1 kg (2 lb) clams
20 g (³/4 oz) unsalted butter
20 g (³/4 oz) plain flour
500 ml (16 fl oz) white wine
1 bay leaf
2 sprigs of fresh thyme
1 tablespoon oil
90 g (3 oz) smoked bacon, cut into cubes
1 onion, chopped
2 celery sticks, sliced
120 g (4 oz) potatoes, cut into small cubes
185 ml (6 fl oz) thick (double) cream
1 teaspoon fresh flat-leaf parsley, shredded

1 Rinse the clams under running water two or three times to remove as much grit as possible. Drain.
2 Melt the butter in a large saucepan over low heat. Add the flour and mix with a whisk or a wooden spoon and cook for 3 minutes. Set aside and allow to cool.

3 Add the wine, bay leaf and thyme to a large stockpot, bring to the boil and cook for 5 minutes over medium heat. Add the clams, cover and simmer for 5–7 minutes, or until the clams have opened. Strain, keeping the cooking liquid for later, and discard any clams that did not open. Set the remaining clams aside to cool. Once cooled, remove from their shells, chop up and set aside.
4 Strain the cooking liquid again through a fine sieve into the pan with the butter and flour mixture. Whisk together, place over medium heat and simmer for about 10 minutes, skimming the top twice, and then set aside.
5 In a large stockpot, heat the oil over medium heat and cook the bacon for 5 minutes, or until nicely coloured. Reduce the heat, add the onion, cover and cook, without colouring, for 3 minutes. Add the celery and cook, covered, for 6 minutes, then add the potato and cook, covered, for 3 minutes. Pour in the thickened clam liquid, cover and simmer for 15–20 minutes, or until the potatoes are just done. Add the chopped clams and the cream and simmer for 5 minutes. Serve the soup sprinkled with the parsley.

Chef's tip Shellfish can contain lots of sand and grit. Always rinse several times, using lots of running water.

Pumpkin soup

Pumpkins are winter squashes, native to America. Their golden colour and firm texture makes them perfect in soups, and the lemon grass gives a tangy taste to cut their sweet flavour.

Preparation time **30 minutes**
Total cooking time **45 minutes**
Serves 6

750 g–I kg (I¹/₂ lb–2 lb) pumpkin
3 large potatoes, chopped
3 large tomatoes, halved and seeded
**I stalk lemon grass, white part only, bruised with the
  side of a large knife**
**1.2 litres chicken stock (see page 62), vegetable stock
  or water**
I¹/₂ tablespoons long-grain rice
pinch of nutmeg
15 g (¹/₂ oz) unsalted butter, optional
3 tablespoons thick (double) cream

1 Cut a wide circle around the pumpkin stem using a small, sharp, pointed knife and remove the top. Using a large metal spoon, scrape the seeds from the pumpkin and discard, then either scrape as much flesh as possible from the pumpkin using the spoon or cut the pumpkin into wedges. Slice just inside the skin to release the flesh and chop it roughly.

2 Place the pumpkin, potato, tomato and lemon grass into a large saucepan with the stock or water. Season with salt and black pepper to taste. Bring to the boil, then reduce the heat and simmer for 25–30 minutes, or until the potatoes are soft. Remove the lemon grass stalk and discard.

3 While the soup is simmering, add the rice to a pan of boiling salted water and stir to the boil. Cook for about 12 minutes, or until tender. Drain the rice in a sieve and rinse under water. Set aside and leave to drain well.

4 Transfer the soup to a blender or food processor and purée until smooth. Return the soup to a clean pan, add the nutmeg and adjust the seasoning. The soup should be thick, but still drinkable from a spoon. If the consistency seems too thick, add a little milk. Stir in the rice, butter and cream, then heat through. Pour into bowls and garnish with freshly ground black pepper and some herbs if desired.

Vichyssoise

A creamy chilled leek and potato soup created in the United States. Instead of leeks, you can use mild Spanish onions. This soup can also be served hot.

Preparation time **25 minutes + 2 hours chilling**
Total cooking time **40 minutes**
Serves 4

30 g (1 oz) unsalted butter
3 large leeks, white part only, finely sliced
1 celery stick, finely sliced
150 g (5 oz) potatoes, chopped into cubes
1 litre chicken stock (see page 62)
100 ml (3¼ fl oz) thick (double) cream
50 ml (1¾ fl oz) cream, for whipping
1 tablespoon fresh chives, chopped

1 Place the butter in a large pan and melt over low heat. Add the leek and celery and cover with buttered greaseproof paper. Cook, without allowing to colour and stirring occasionally, for 15 minutes, or until soft. Add the potatoes and stock and season to taste with salt and freshly ground black pepper.

2 Bring the soup to the boil, then reduce the heat and simmer for 15 minutes, or until the potatoes become very soft. Purée the soup in batches in a food processor or blender, pour into a bowl, stir in the cream and season with salt and pepper. Cover with plastic wrap and allow to cool before placing in the refrigerator to chill for at least 2 hours.

3 Serve the soup in chilled bowls. Spoon some semi-whipped cream onto the centre of the soup and sprinkle with chives to garnish.

Summer prawn and cucumber soup

An unusual and refreshing soup with its origins in the Middle East. Very easy to make, it should be served chilled, accompanied by flat bread, for a perfect alfresco lunch.

*Preparation time **20 minutes + 30 minutes standing + 2–3 hours refrigeration***
*Total cooking time **10 minutes***
Serves 6–8

250 g (8 oz) cucumber
1 egg, optional
375 ml (12 fl oz) chicken stock (see page 62)
155 ml (5 fl oz) tomato juice
2 x 450 g (14¼ oz) cartons Greek-style or plain yoghurt
125 ml (4 fl oz) cream
60 g (2 oz) cooked shelled prawns, fresh or frozen, coarsely chopped
12 medium cooked prawns, shells on
1 clove garlic, crushed
1 teaspoon chopped fresh mint
1 teaspoon chopped fresh chives

1 Peel and cut the cucumber into 1 cm (1/2 inch) cubes, salt them lightly and leave on a plate for about 30 minutes. Rinse under cold water, drain and dry on crumpled paper towels.

2 Bring a small pan of salted water to the boil, lower in the egg and simmer for 7 minutes. Lift the egg out into a bowl of iced water to stop the cooking process and tap to just crack the shell. Leave in the water until just cool enough to remove the shell, then return the egg to the cold water. When fully cooled, chop roughly.

3 In a large bowl, mix the chicken stock, tomato juice and yoghurt together. When quite smooth, add the cucumber, cream and chopped prawns to the soup. Season to taste with salt and freshly ground black pepper. Cover and place in the refrigerator to chill for 2–3 hours.

4 Meanwhile, remove the shell from the whole prawns, leaving the heads and tails on, then devein them. Cover and store in the refrigerator.

5 Rub the soup bowls with the garlic. Pour in the soup and sprinkle with the egg and chopped mint and chives. Hang two prawns on the side of each bowl and serve immediately, accompanied by fresh bread.

Chef's tip To keep a hard-boiled egg from overcooking, it must be cooled immediately in iced water. The quick cooling also prevents an unsightly greeny grey ring from forming around the yolk.

Apple and parsnip soup

Don't save your fruit for dessert—a fruit and vegetable soup makes a wonderful beginning to a meal. Granny Smiths are just right for this recipe as they are not too sweet.

*Preparation time **30 minutes***
*Total cooking time **40 minutes***
Serves 6

30 g (1 oz) unsalted butter
1 onion, chopped
2 celery sticks, chopped
5 parsnips, chopped
3 Granny Smith apples, or similar variety,
**   peeled and chopped**
bouquet garni (see page 63)
1.5 litres chicken stock (see page 62)
a few sprigs of fresh thyme, to garnish
chopped walnuts, to garnish

1 Heat the butter in a medium saucepan, add the onion, cover with buttered greaseproof paper and a lid and cook gently until the onion is transparent, but not coloured. Add the celery, parsnip and apple and season with salt and pepper. Cook for a few minutes, then add the bouquet garni and cover with the chicken stock.

2 Bring to the boil, then reduce the heat and simmer for 25 minutes, or until the vegetables are soft. Skim the surface, remove the bouquet garni, transfer the soup to a food processor or blender and process until smooth. Return the soup to a clean saucepan, reseason to taste and reheat.

3 Divide the soup into bowls. Arrange a little thyme and some chopped walnuts in the centre of each soup to serve.

Chef's tip For a different garnish, stir 1 tablespoon of Calvados into 100 ml (3¹/4 fl oz) thick (double) cream. Carefully swirl the flavoured cream into the soup just before serving.

Chef's techniques

◆

Making fish stock

Use white fish, rather than oily fish such as salmon, trout or mackerel. Remove the eyes and gills.

Place 2 kg (4 lb) chopped fish bones and trimmings in salted water for 10 minutes; drain. Return to a clean pan with 2.5 litres water, 12 peppercorns, 2 bay leaves, chopped celery stick and onion and juice of 1 lemon.

Bring to the boil, then reduce the heat and simmer for 20 minutes. During simmering, skim off any scum that rises to the surface using a large spoon.

Ladle the stock in batches into a fine sieve over a bowl. Gently press the solids with a ladle to extract all the liquid and place in the refrigerator to cool. Makes 1.5 litres.

Making chicken stock

Good, flavoursome home-made stock can be the cornerstone of a great soup.

Cut up 750 g (1 1/2 lb) chicken bones and carcass and put in a pan with a roughly chopped onion, carrot and celery stick. Add 6 peppercorns, a bouquet garni and 4 litres water.

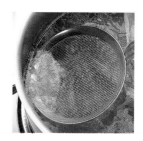

Bring to the boil and let the stock simmer gently for 2–3 hours, skimming off any scum that rises to the surface using a large spoon. Strain the stock through a sieve into a clean bowl, then allow to cool.

Chill the stock overnight, then lift off any fat. If you can't leave overnight, drag the surface of the hot strained stock with paper towels to lift off the fat. Makes 1.5–2 litres.

Making brown stock

Roasting the bones gives a good colour to the stock and helps to remove the excess fat.

Roast 1.5 kg (3 lb) beef or veal bones at very hot 230°C (450°F/Gas 8) for 40 minutes, adding a quartered onion, 2 chopped carrots, 1 chopped leek and 1 chopped celery stick halfway through.

Transfer to a clean pan. Add 4 litres water, 2 tablespoons tomato paste, bouquet garni and 6 peppercorns. Simmer for 3–4 hours, skimming often.

Ladle the stock in batches into a fine sieve over a bowl. Gently press the solids with the ladle to extract all the liquid and place in the refrigerator to cool. Lift off any fat. Makes 1.5–2 litres.

Clarifying butter

Removing the water and solids from butter makes it less likely to burn. Ghee is a form of clarified butter.

To make 100 g (3 1/4 oz) clarified butter, cut 180 g (5 3/4 oz) butter into small cubes. Place in a small pan set into a larger pot of water over low heat. Melt the butter without stirring.

Remove the pan from the heat and allow to cool slightly. Skim the foam from the surface, being careful not to stir the butter.

Pour off the clear yellow liquid, being very careful to leave the milky sediment behind in the pan. Discard the sediment and store the clarified butter in an airtight container in the refrigerator.

Freezing stock

Stock will keep in the refrigerator for 3 days. It can be frozen in portions for later use, for 6 months.

After removing any fat, boil the stock until reduced to 500 ml (16 fl oz). Cool and freeze until solid. Transfer to a plastic bag and seal. To make 2 litres stock, add 1.5 litres water to 500 ml (16 fl oz) concentrated stock.

Bouquet garni

Add the flavour and aroma of herbs to your dish with a freshly made bouquet garni.

Wrap the green part of a leek loosely around a bay leaf, a sprig of thyme, some celery leaves and a few stalks of parsley, then tie with string. Leave a long tail to the string for easy removal.

Published by Murdoch Books® a division of Murdoch Magazines Pty Limited, 213 Miller Street, North Sydney NSW 2060.

Murdoch Books and Le Cordon Bleu thank the 32 masterchefs of all the Le Cordon Bleu Schools, whose knowledge and expertise have made this book possible, especially: Chef Cliche (MOF), Chef Terrien, Chef Boucheret, Chef Duchêne (MOF), Chef Guillut, Chef Steneck, Paris; Chef Males, Chef Walsh, Chef Hardy, London; Chef Chantefort, Chef Bertin, Chef Jambert, Chef Honda, Tokyo; Chef Salembien, Chef Boutin, Chef Harris, Sydney; Chef Lawes, Adelaide; Chef Guiet, Chef Denis, Ottawa. Of the many students who helped the Chefs test each recipe, a special mention to graduates David Welch and Allen Wertheim. A very special acknowledgment to Directors Susan Eckstein, Great Britain, and Kathy Shaw, Paris, who have been responsible for the coordination of the Le Cordon Bleu team throughout this series.

Murdoch Books®
Managing Editor: Kay Halsey
Series Concept, Design and Art Direction: Juliet Cohen
Food Director: Jody Vassallo
Food Editors: Lulu Grimes, Kathy Knudsen, Tracy Rutherford
Designer: Annette Fitzgerald
Photographer: Joe Filshie
Food Stylist: Carolyn Fienberg
Food Preparation: Jo Forrest
Chef's Techniques Photographer: Reg Morrison
Home Economists: Michelle Lawton, Kerrie Mullins, Kerrie Ray

CEO & Publisher: Anne Wilson
Publishing Director: Catie Ziller
General Manager: Mark Smith
Creative Director: Marylouise Brammer
International Sales Director: Mark Newman

National Library of Australia Cataloguing-in-Publication Data
Soups. ISBN 0 86411 735 3. 1. Soups. (Series: Le Cordon Bleu home collection). 641.813

Printed by Toppan Printing (S) Pte Ltd
First Printed 1997
©Design and photography Murdoch Books® 1997
©Text Le Cordon Bleu 1997

Distributed in the UK by D Services, 6 Euston Street, Freemen's Common, Leicester LE2 7SS Tel 0116-254-7671 Fax 0116-254-4670. Distributed in Canada by Whitecap (Vancouver) Ltd, 351 Lynn Avenue, North Vancouver, BC V7J 2C4 Tel 604-980-9852 Fax 604-980-8197 or Whitecap (Ontario) Ltd, 47 Coldwater Road, North York, ON M3B 1Y8 Tel 416-444-3442 Fax 416-444-6630

The Publisher and Le Cordon Bleu wish to thank Carole Sweetnam for her help with this series.
Front cover: New England clam chowder

IMPORTANT INFORMATION

CONVERSION GUIDE

1 cup = 250 ml (8 fl oz)
1 Australian tablespoon = 20 ml (4 teaspoons)
1 UK tablespoon = 15 ml (3 teaspoons)

NOTE: We have used 20 ml tablespoons. If you are using a 15 ml tablespoon, for most recipes the difference will be negligible. For recipes using baking powder, gelatine, bicarbonate of soda and flour, add an extra teaspoon for each tablespoon specified.

CUP CONVERSIONS—DRY INGREDIENTS

1 cup flour, plain or self-raising = 125 g (4 oz)
1 cup sugar, caster = 250 g (8 oz)
1 cup breadcrumbs, dry = 125 g (4 oz)

IMPORTANT: Those who might be at risk from the effects of salmonella food poisoning (the elderly, pregnant women, young children and those suffering from immune deficiency diseases) should consult their GP with any concerns about eating raw eggs.